WHEN IS A BURNING TREE

Poems By
Christina Seymour

GLASS LYRE PRESS

Copyright © 2018 Christina Seymour
Paperback ISBN: 978-1-941783-53-5

All rights reserved: except for the purpose of quoting brief passages for review, no part of this book may be reproduced or transmitted in any form or by any means, electronic or mechanical, including photocopying, recording, or by any information storage and retrieval system, without permission in writing from the publisher.

Cover art: "I Am on a Lonely Road and I Am Traveling"
            by Eileen Shaloum
Design & layout: Steven Asmussen
Copyediting: Linda E. Kim

Glass Lyre Press, LLC
P.O. Box 2693
Glenview, IL 60025
www.GlassLyrePress.com

Contents

Acknowledgements	vii
Covered Wagon Trail	1
Stage-Struck	2
Colors of Mountains and Grass Are Tears	4
Lattice of Leaves Above Me	5
Let Me Make This Painless	6
Injured Bird Loop	7
New House: Brick with Lime Green Door	8
My Business	9
Now: Bright Towel on Sand	10

***

Grace	13
Land of Amber Sky	14
Dear Muse,	15
Live Flower Necklace	16
Inferiority: An Underwater Dance of Lights	17
Two Omens Inside the Amber Alert	18
A Kind of Goodbye	19

***

Gray Steam Before Lightning   23

***

Watercolor Fox, Patience	31
Symphony Orchestra	32
Yes, it's been this long.	33
Bones Picked Fuchsia	34
Rain on the Roof	35
New Tree by the Reservoir	36
From which *No* comes this mourning?	37
Busy Trying	38
You, Me, and the Problem	39
Spark in a Pile of Leaves	40

***

Craft Scissor Ridge	43
Third Day of No Good News	44
Natural Graves	45
Mid-Day Hail	46
Pajama Drawer of Adolescence	47
To Feel as Real as Each New Morning	48
Lime Dogwood on Gray Sky	49

***

Broken Pot I Made	53
Not Knowing What to Say	54
all the salt swelling of the sea laughed aloud	55
When We Look Out from the Pier	56
Addition and Subtraction	57
Logic as I Know It	58

Cages for Plovers	59
Plans	60
Floor Findings	61
Meanwhile, our Snowman Melts	62
Truth Color	63
About the Author	65

Acknowledgements

Arsenic Lobster: "Land of Amber Sky" and "Live Flower Necklace"

The Briar Cliff Review: "Stage-Struck"

Cider Press Review: "Grace"

HitchLit Review: "*all the salt swelling of the sea laughed aloud,*" "Inferiority: An Underwater Dance of Lights," and "Watercolor Fox, Patience"

The Moth: "New House: Brick with Lime Green Door"

North American Review: "Channel Inn Balcony" (text appears in "Gray Steam Before Lightning")

Structo: "Addition and Subtraction" appears in the chapbook *Flowers Around Your Soft Throat*

Third Wednesday: "It's Just a Dark Hill" (text appears in "Gray Steam Before Lightning")

Covered Wagon Trail
after Ophelia *by Sir John Everett Millais*

Swift creekwater swells over her thin muscles, virgin heart,
a must-see curiosity, backdrop of trees, stricken blue,

pink roses brightened to funeral-level. I constantly pull
my hound away from her bravery: *what might the scorpion*

by the verbena taste like? These woods are a burial ground
for the once-found-and-lost-again: there lies the horse statue,

king of wet dirt, the bear statue holding church for stones.
Here lies the spinning squirrel, who fell from a nut tree

beside the mini-golf course we played last night. You felt
somewhere else. I, lately, pity. This is Ophelia,

not *unrequited* but in a stage of giving up, eyes open
but fixed inward on something far and earnest, a crown

dismantled by water. Wilted blue and yellow buds graze
her unforced hands like obsessions that summon.

Stage-Struck

1.

Gathering the loose strings of last night's argument,
I try to remember what I believe—
the silken bark that moss commits to—
even the beginning of coping, even with lost hands.

I create you over and over, to perfect light behind trees,
unlike the possible simplicity of cutting out squirrel shapes in kindergarten.
My father offers, *You are equal to life* and *Inspiration is not gone from you.*

2.

Starry Night Over the Rhone made music of my lost temperament: its stringy whites and carpet blues shared that moment of dissonance between us. It said, *I understand you, both of you,* and silence let our claims fall like worn sheets, cotton-frayed, feather-light, and finally the sun receded to make just one mountain visible—the hook-topped one—the godly nose of something immoveable but present. The parting of my lips gives room for two new, shiny objects to enter—forgiveness and light.

3.

When I hold your hand without hesitation, I mean to say,
why must the carousel be a metaphor for relentlessness?
I mean to say, *maybe if we just try.*

On a spontaneous weekend trip to the beach,
I search for the you from *before*—

as we watch the sand disappear under the tide,
I settle for the sea. I keep my unsayable sadness:
I hope that hope, a small beach fire made from our hands, will come.

Colors of Mountains and Grass Are Tears

after With Open Arms *by Eileen Shaloum*

In the Monet-like border,
a white dock leads to my childhood house:
the wall of trees makes a jail with blacked-out windows
that hide people playing cards, people having words,
people driving away, people crying.

If I am in the painting, I must be in my room,
envisioning lips on the bunk bed above me,
the lips of a spirit-me whose eyes
are cut by an invisible line so that
one closed shadow-eye weeps toward the house,
and the other gazes at the alien steeples
on tops of mirrored buildings in the city:

some windows are circles, and some are squares.
Why would I, a central floating figure,
reach through a book called *Wide Open*
to my other mannequin-arm that tries
to console me but can't bend that way?

My bottom disappears into pink bulls-eye flowers—
I am almost a mermaid—almost dead—
almost rising out of the fire of the sun,
dotted along my thigh. The fuchsia lake below me is stamped
with block letters that rearrange and repeat a cliché.

Lattice of Leaves Above Me

In the center of the chamber of trees,
I am a target for bugs. A black spider falls

onto a page of my book, onto the word *target*,
and to have noticed is both special and lonely.

RV campers decorate awnings with blue rope-lights
as a way to be seen in the dark.

An aerial view might show a cluster of neon domes,
ballooned with mist of multiple blankets and breath,

a few muted clouds of tree-tufts and smoke.
I settle into the *might-not-have-been* or the *never-was*

as our wedding song plays on a wind-up radio.
Missing you takes over, and then the other story:

the way we hadn't dealt with all we needed to.
I remember kicking a ball between two trees

as a child, catching a long-legged spider
and removing its legs because their bodies

were useless poison: like each limb chain-sawed
by the city workers—*not that tree*, I shout,

that plays *risk* with black wires, *not that limb*
that has always blocked me from being seen.

Let Me Make This Painless

During our back-and-forth, I imagine
Winslow Homer smearing white and navy—

his placement of the red man: *blink*.
Red man: *hold a tool*.

Red man: a bold, immovable streak.
You and I stand on opposite sides

of the cart of groceries
saying what exactly could be different—

we could be the fiery sea that tosses the red man: still.
We could be the anchor of the dark-everything,

the small decision of sunlight that was planned.
But we fail again to listen,

beep our beets and toilet paper through the machine,
our two brains propped on the fragile trunks of our bodies,

called, in the world of a painting,
the focal point, our meaning relative to mood.

Injured Bird Loop

Small, I watched my father cup the injured pigeon
in the Buick's grille like an easily bruised fruit.
Today, a lark sways, sick, over a marble surface
of purple grass and bee-swarmed piles
of composite wood left from some abandoned project:
a tree house, maybe, for a child never wanting it,
or a restoration of a historic cabin, unfunded.

One-and-only is a fiction I keep investing in—
scraps of dreams before me like this. As the deer
who tentatively crosses this meadow, then bolts
at the explosion of rustling feathers on leaves,
I treat molehills as craters to dodge, test my care
against the sweet, perfect beads of lavender:
trying, gently, I am just a single waving hand.

New House: Brick with Lime Green Door

Flames like white slugs, coals like a red-hot maple,
spring casts its forgiving sun over every wave of the river.

The mosquito leaves a button of blood on my arm
and one argyle leg in the pile of sap, as a reminder of fragility.

In the butterfly garden: a crimson for every mood;
the *everywhere* of the robin's chuckle when it fills silence.

Couplets offer enough space to hold our separateness:
your sweet determination, my eyes diverted.

As a child, I must have desired such worry,
pretend-smoking a pretzel stick or pulling weeds from brick.

Now, engines chug to picnics or flowery grave sites.
Tonight, our faces change over each scene of the movie:

how communal our winces and smiles;
how private our thoughts of this place—

the crawlspace, already overrun by cave crickets. You must
wonder if I'm all right as much as I wonder if you are.

My Business

There's only so much preparing
for the flood of acorns, their soft meat
crumbled in piles on the sidewalk,
for the next time you might lie.
This is the less we talked about:
one covered branch shakes
from an unseen crow. The signs
are there. I don't listen. Instead,
I let her leash get caught
to have something to untangle;
I park under the apple blossom
to pick wet petals
from my windshield.
I must not be made for the arc
of a normal day, stuck between two,
large Rothko-style paint strokes:
putting off the morning and wondering
if I am wanted. Let me sift through
the clouds of worry and smirking
crows to get to myself—the one
sweeping acorns to signify defeat.

Now: Bright Towel on Sand

Four gulls join me on the beach to look the same direction,
toward the shirtless, singing guy on the bike,

brave enough to be loud, a reminder
of parties where I drive you home in a silence

you don't notice. Self-deception is the concrete storm
before me, one gull turning its beak like a lighthouse,

surveying my progress, as I select
from the beach a white clam shell with a peach,

airbrushed pinky-print like that of a child, like me
who selected, too, personalities while playing House—

the one-who-wears-an-apron or the one-who-is-loved-
by-many-men. I was saying to myself:

you will do for my project of keeping you or giving you away.
Now: a waxy seabird's uncaring stance.

* * *

GRACE

So what of this empty street, new blank fridge,
old pictures waiting to be hung?

Here is the same *before:* bluejays, steeple clouds, darkening
over shuttered houses and rusty cars in yards.

Each night, crickets know the value of a repetitive task;
cicadas send clicks to the lemon-rind edge of the moon.

Not one but two tire swings hang from the shattered maple
in the neighbor's yard, part of spinning we never give up.

Since it hurts not to, being-with-you must be compulsive,
a respite from a heavy sigh that can't be lifted.

After that realization, it's always the same way home, past this little fear,
a loose cat in the alley—the progress of one canvas sky to another:

the firefly is a worthwhile cliché, the way wings lift before body,
or the earthworm, with its two sexes and five impossible hearts.

Land of Amber Sky

This is a fact: Gracie trails her ears through dandelions, returns with white wisps on her eyelids.

I think, for this, she deserves the name Andromeda, the potential for gold in the ordinary.

As I try to take a picture, she grabs the decomposing rabbit's foot she's had on her mind for days.

Sometimes, the key to believing your worth is letting truth in.

It will be the right time, I think, considering whether or not I will accept love.

He has been there, saying it. I have been faithless out of self-protection.

Searching for connection is like clearing away litter from Central Park's *Imagine* mosaic;

picking a used toothpick or shard of glass off of a black-and-white rainbow.

Maybe the gods-of-me say, *she's responding well to thunder* one day and *she needs less* the next.

It's important to watch the season change: fat birds pick at all the new buds, sending their faces to the sun.

Dear Muse,

You are not my face, my body, nor what people expect,
One-eyed Barred Owl, shivering over the firefly-lit backyard—

the teal blow-up pool that bugs died in,
our muddy bike path around the brick city-block.

You followed me when my brother and I rode opposite ways
to high-five in the middle—

when I was alone but racing,
racing but wondering where he was.

A spider reaches over the fire-pit's rim with its thready legs
to be sure there is another side.

You are doing this around my insides, quietly.
You are the sap-circle surface of the tree stump

that my neighbor often mentions grinding to nothing
and that one day, I tasted. It's not useless:

inside, I could plant horsemint to draw the bees,
pesky voices that remind me what is really going on.

Live Flower Necklace

What is compulsive, if not the desire
to draw corn on the orange moon,

encircling our distant bodies
on a quiet beach labeled *Honeymoon*.

Coloring inside the lines does not ease
the headache of realization-after-realization.

Silence can be both protective and repressive.
I am not sure which one mine is, yet,

so I clutch both hands, ordinarily,
to turn-up the presence of soft, red

bells sloped toward the ground,
mirrored sand that neutralizes my weight

like a zero-gravity chair. Bands
of dusk paint our faces purple, striped,

and I take a walk alone, which is not alone
so long as I am there—rush of ocean,

shell of horseshoe crab, containers
saving my words for when I am ready.

Inferiority: An Underwater Dance of Lights

Evening spring, white petals turning under—
I want to believe that I feel perfectly safe
on a dark street by the man shouting at his son.
Gracie scrapes at the ground, ignorant, as I yank her forward.

Similar is the sound of a car hovering close behind,
the way a star-filled dusk turns into a moment to escape,
to grip the pepper spray or keys and push ahead.

Later, I force an empty soda bottle under bath water,
feel bubbles float up, over my legs, like a piece of wheat
dragged across the back of the neck. Suds shift
on the surface: the sound of a skirt pulled over nylons.

I feel like a film negative, black-and-white reverse of the original,
a lady bug turned to shell, a lake turned to smoke.
I wish I had a god to tell me *sit still* or *know your worth,*

but I settle for the maternal hare in my imagination, eyelashes
blinking approval—or the real heron with silver feathers
who makes peace with the risk of fishing in the city dam,
startles and billows out at the first clatter of a train.

Two Omens Inside the Amber Alert

Dead rabbit in the yard with its arms and head, gone,
only the torso, only the hangers of its back legs.

Reports said he had groomed her with song,
groomed her by listening.

Then, under the rock on the porch, the salamander rots:
white edges on the turquoise body where legs used to be.

Mid-evening, red sun traces long, dead pines
like fingers that gripped the missing girl,

forest floors combed by feet to find her; a deer stops to sniff
her perfumed hand as it becomes part of the goldenrod.

The rabbit was found first by my dog, who gnawed its neck
like the fox with the white-tipped tail I caught jumping,

blood mark on its mouth. Then, the salamander—she led me to it,
wanting to cover herself in the reek of a lifeless thing.

A Kind of Goodbye

Last year, this time, the local male swan, Romeo, killed Juliet,
so a new Juliet is being introduced, slowly.

Two boys in an unmufflered car interrupt the process
with *fuckings* and *assholes*, the kind of disinterest

of my hometown: traffic and gravel alleys,
corner bars and rusted tracks. The sunset flames behind

the mountain-lined pond, urges the swan-like motion
of one hand to reach for another, to grip the slingshot-

middle of the honeysuckle and soak it into my skin:
a salve for noise, the antithesis of *eye-roll*. To urge, itself,

is a kind of answer: the dead phlox that we planted together
does not worry about whether or not it will come back.

* * *

Gray Steam Before Lightning

"The well-built palace was filled with light, as if from a flash of lightning."

—*"Homeric Hymn to Demeter," trans. Gregory Nagy*

I.

Backdrop of rusted cars in yards, soft triangle mountains,
I wonder if I am always *the* passenger or always *yours*

on the drive through farmland, old tourist attractions,
where people mined for gems, where one lamb always hides in the back,

where the aspen leaf dies its particular way, flirtation
of yellow and green, then brown, like an injured bird, flakes.

When I say, *where are we*, you say, *not there yet*.
I wonder what permission you need to begin looking,

why the woodpecker, offering its sweet red to the world,
feels more right for me than you—if that would be the case with anyone.

II.

It's no one's fault: the way you smiled but didn't in your school picture,
having just been pelted with snow, your mouth, crowded with marbles,
worry in your silence—silence, my own way of being useful.

At times, I don't know which of my hands smooths your back in the sigh
of midnight, or which *yes* is really a *yes*. A pincushion reminds me of our bed,
our toothpick limbs twisted with twine. Clumsy, I want to touch my cheek

to your back. I want to protect you from waking. I know that *good-enough*,
several times a day, is hope misfiring,
one white stream in the canyon of an eye.

III.

Ready for truth, I paint each slat of the wood chair beet-colored,
with an old brush, thinking: *simply-doing* is the right way, not

waiting for the right way to come along.
Then: rain. Maroon leaks onto the wood deck

like wine pooled on a counter. New wind brings
cracking bullfrogs, my hair stuck to my neck;

I accept that I am not yet good at this—painting; letting go.

IV.

Light flickers on a dying streetlamp
on a dark country road. It owns the sky.
My tongue clicks into the sway of anger,
so round and heavy, I don't believe
it could have come from me.
It's not like anyone asked me delete myself
in service of memory, to hide laughter
in the cavern of a conch shell.
You, like an old t-shirt, waiting
to be rediscovered like swabbing
cotton on a cut; the day we planned
to drive forever, and did,
the way we were so sure.

Then, shock, red spray
in the middle of a white field:
when is a burning tree,
hot against the fog,
painting orange the once-erased:
forest-edges of doubt, tangled cords of roots,
even the tiniest snail gripping rock-face,
dulled, before, by the kind of lie
that begins with certainty.

V.

I run my finger along your spine, want this moment
of us, alone, to equal the sharp wind of petals and rain

that I punched as a child, that I thought I had a chance with.
We are each our own flaw: bugs and strands of hair

hang from shirt pockets. I smooth our smiles
in a photo: waterfalls behind us,

our gaze on some addictive light, a flash of with-ness.
A 19th century spirit photograph superimposes

an image of the dead on a family photo of the living—
a crafty fulfillment of longing. Monarchs collect

on the last branch of the season, sink it closer
to the ground. To be as defined, I outline my own sections

with a black felt-tipped marker, then circle the cracks
of the rotten tree, on our foreheads: targets of time to be tended.

VI.

Dew flicking my ankles, I return
with a new understanding—
you are a vulnerable creature, too—
a darkened under eye, a pinched cheek,
a brow not with *lines* of stress but muscles
like soft caterpillars found their shadows there.
In listening, I am a black butterfly
that steps on each fin of dandelion,
crunching lightly clouds of yellow.
I can guess at the source—a young boy
suturing his own skinned knee,
that I might have made you lonely, too.
We will always have both
the sting of our bitten lips
and the copper glow of pennies,
thrown from our hands as children.
While the murky green of the pond
is not the blue beach we wished for,
wind still lifts our hair; salt balms
as it would near any ocean.

VII.

Red dots of a runway trace the black channel
like the loneliness of being sung to.
You left for food, angry.

Boats seem to listen with their nightlight light,
poised for city-people who shower behind glass
that no one looks through.

In one of the portholes, the size of my thumbnail,
credits to a movie roll: cello and drums must fill
the docked boat, now, my head, as we wait

for the night to do something about *sorry*.

VIII.

Collected and pinned above the horizon,
the moon is the vapor of a gold breath.
I followed you up a clamber of stones
to get to the top of this mountain city,
to say we did, to face every cast shadow
that could hide a black bear. Beside me,
you are familiar and foreign at once.
Feeling your feeling is how I lost myself;
let us stick to driving separately to the ledge
before the stars, where we meet back
in the parking lot, pink light, blue ridge,
artificial fluorescents, too hot to touch
but warm with energy, the way a firefly,
glows for a moment after death,
only no longer looking like magic.

VIIII.

Something-missing does not solve itself
in the magazine-collage sunset on a weekend trip,
though its edges give shape to silence.

I remember we didn't set out milk
for the alley cat who keeps returning
to our feet when we check the mail;

when I tell you, I really look:
your tired eyes ripe with sorrow
that you've grown in distance,

my own fingers raw from fixing.
Then: a gray ladybug on my arm
for just enough time to say, *let's wish*—

let us wish that we are out of wishes,
that our faces be our faces.

* * *

Watercolor Fox, Patience
after Fire Spirit *by Luqman Reza Mulyono*

The one orange room
is because of the sunrise,
just as I am *because*.

Answers fall short of the gray
swirls of the painted fox,
just as this speech is as silent

as sitting near an evening fir,
watching wood flake to wind.
We want always for the warmth

to make sense of distance:
quiet night against croaking animals,
your way of changing subjects.

Family prefers me cushioned by snow,
drawing wings rather than
no, not yet, no. When I cup

a golden puddle of broken ice
by a muddy river with gloved hands,
it is a steadiness like being held.

Muses can grow from gravel
in the coldest air of the season.
There is no *dust to dust*.

There is no sleight of hand.

Symphony Orchestra

The jade sunset doesn't hum. It casts its somber
sway over the city, crowded wooden bars

where men yell bands' biographies, women
perch in their seats, clarinets perched at their knees.

Winter reminds how my memory is softer than truth:
frosted windowpane vs. the numb ankles of reality.

Today, the recently divorced, I imagine, shut doors
of their children's rooms and wait until it feels right

to move on. The horn player reaches inside the brass tulip,
cradling sound like the sputtering heart of an injured bird.

I feel it's my job to settle the questions of a somber crowd,
but notes on the staff remind me: earlier, the black mesh screen

that framed the forest that I deemed *beautiful*
held dozens of bugs, stuck, waving—

Yes, it's been this long.

The hole in you comes up for breath
in the form of your gnarled throat: bronchitis.
Your isolation is a cove that cuts against
my wanting to give you a bath to bring your fever down,
sponge rivulets down your spine.

Because I know this is loving-beyond,
I kick rocks on the street, instead,
lead Gracie through the duff in our yard,
turn over leaves to look for lizards,
find one dead among glass shards from previous owners,
who broke beer bottles on the edge of the concrete fire pit.

I don't feel interesting enough to deserve you,
or anyone—
the moment of myself, alone, in the hideaway space
in the woods with the garbaged microwave
and the quiet turtle with no home
is what I've been fleeing my whole life, it seems.

Bones Picked Fuchsia
after The Pink Bird Corridor *by Soren James*

The skull of the pink bird once contoured a brain
that learned to mimic our primate habits: she tips her toe
nonchalantly as if in front of a blue corridor of mirrors

as I do when judging the worth of a new piece of jewelry.
Her picked-clean ribcage makes my own feel breakable
as if at any moment my breath could surge through

the polygons of a dark dream, gasp snapping clavicle.
I would have picked her up if I found her squawking
on a beachfront, moved her to covered dunes,

but she is stronger than me—standing relaxed before my gaze.
Her marbled wing-bone is a sturdy fin in a smear of ocean.
In the black hole of her once-eye: pastel shapes of possibility.

Rain on the Roof

The first day of spring brought rain, a midday dream
of mountain goats gathered on craggy, mossy stone.
As I inched closer, they scattered under an atmosphere of trees.

This is the weariness of another year, a new facial line.
Which shade of lipstick should I wear to step over
piles of muddy hay beside the gently melting duck pond?
Go the Distance, Wonderstruck, Niagara Overlook?

As much as it doesn't matter, it does—
which disappointment to cover, to stand myself,
which power to call on for awakening.

During the thaw, the neighborhood kitten slept in the ditch pipe,
curled against her own warmth, eyes shut with hope.
I crowded my heart with resistance—blue clapping thunder—
and am waiting until she survives every frost to release it.

New Tree by the Reservoir

I tell worth, *I am full of potential, at least.*
It is normal to walk through brambles, unsure.

Any living thing is as good as a Renoir: the way
the lawn changes: diagonal light green to dark;

blades dance, almost whistle, lift;
dandelions float against midnight.

I told the tulip, earlier, I was sorry I couldn't love it,
and now I am saying, *but look, I still can.*

My pink hand in the cool, gray river
and the rusty teal bridge we once agreed about

give full shape to *always-used-to-be*—
how fire's rage renews the forest floor.

From which *No* comes this mourning?

Little Miss Helpful, the blond pink circle of a girl,
teaches that helping can make things worse:

trip Mr. Tall while tying his shoes, destroy
Mr. Happy's home while trying to cure him.

During boys' baseball games, I dug through gravel,
walked loops, left sticks like breadcrumbs

back to the person I was the day before.
After evening shifts, my mom removed her nylons,

tired and stressed. New bruises on my knees
mirrored the lilacs I arranged in a water glass

for her approval. Soon: no more fishing or shirtless
games of kickball, sheets no longer decorated

with sweat and grass. Which parts of me, still,
listen to an invisible voice, saying, *Behave*?

Busy Trying

My artifacts: one wrinkled eyelid, a lip stained with a scar,
and a second imagination, for all the *not-wanting-to-know*.

This mulchy path weaves into the static of woods;
my desire for completeness, a pile of green apples, rotting.

What do crows shout to god while perched on the hollow wood
of the dead aspen, such an unsteady ground for wanting?

Do they send signals of loss, searching for suitable mates?
Do they wing into stratosphere, trying to touch

the red balloon, escaped from a child's loose grip on her birthday,
before it shrivels into a tangle of what it used to be?

I press on, through the thicket—time's aching *what-to-do-today*—
and relinquish my locket to the branch that took it, tired already.

You, Me, and the Problem

Of course, a squirrel still leaps through tall grass.
Cardinals parse dirt from twigs.
At the breakfast table, I feel we are unfixable,
your fears, my fears, lain on sheets together
after coming to bed at separate times,
heads turned forcefully ahead.

Still, by full-on morning, crickets play their legs.
Sun gathers behind a soft sidewalk of clouds.
An orchid climbing a mailbox reminds me,
vanilla bean is born from it—lips grip cups stained pink,
a smattering of sweet, black beans—
disappointment, born from an ancestral dark,
disappointment, born from the very first breath.

Spark in a Pile of Leaves

Surging, several-day wildfire reminds me how little
I can do to hurt, or help. From inside the hotel, windows

normally framing mountains frame flames—
manic dancers stripping trees. There is no

pretend you are okay; no *look for proof of strength*.
After: a broken mirror in black ash—

its stubborn inability to lie, its thick, unheroic glass—
reflects cracked trunks, the first jewels of rain,

red clouds in my eyes from a day of not knowing.
I start to say, *I am fire, too*, in the silver stripe of sputtered

aluminum, but the unabashed haze corrects: I cannot expect
to be equal to force nor to have any idea what's next.

***

CRAFT SCISSOR RIDGE
after Gas, 1940 *by Edward Hopper*

Highlighted crack of sky on brick—
I learned to stop wanting,
which is why I am impatient
with too much talk.
Hollow twigs shuffle from tree
to ground like how I neglected
a dream, settled into a briefcase
of time and peered out only
to check the status. The low-lying
motel is the something-different
that is needed. Blind slats show
in-between, as in our separation,
motel bed to motel bed. Between us,
years pass like a half-second,
and I feel like nothing brilliant, just one
of many names on a screen. Attention
can be shared but not always
communicated: the sliver of moon
over the neon green and red gas station.
In the parking lot: a tiny curl of pink yarn
from an heirloom doll's head, I imagine,
a remnant that must have been part
of *here* for awhile, through all types
of weather: spring tornado, winter
frost, the current humidity,
however sticky, that cradles
the way we all once were.

Third Day of No Good News

Winged seeds and white petals design my windshield each morning.

Grip on the steering wheel, I wipe them away without noticing, or let the wind take them.

This is a new season: here, the same feelings as I had them last year, *only we aren't telling*,

says the same broken-mirror sun on the brown mountain.

The neighborhood rooster takes on the responsibility of sending a signal:

change is slow and mostly internal, cautious steps in black water.

The sweet leaf skates a large, reflective puddle, a paper boat on a purple swirl of grease and rain.

An ambulance siren shrieks through the forest for three whole, long minutes.

Then, still, the leaf, still. That, itself, is a secret.

Natural Graves

She's brought me souvenirs from the cemetery,
the man says about the stray dog.
Which of my bones would I not mind
being taken? Maybe a joint in my little finger,
one rib-bone, or a part of my lower leg,
whatever would allow me to stay collected
in a stained glass pattern around my absent organs—
the feeling of sun-on-bone, light casting shadow,
like fish lipping algae from dishes in a small cave.

A woman, on a distant island,
might be working out similar plans for her body.
Her island feels welcoming to tourists
but not those who grew up there, like her—
memories of parked cars in certain lots
or taunting voices in certain parks
she speeds by to get to the sugar fields.
We chose to hide certain parts of ourselves:
beige skin under different beige, ash hair under red;
one more meal to skip to be a zero.

Carcass of the fox shows that limbs taken
cannot be replaced, totally, but that light
will try to make a new foot with a shadow,
turquoise, to match her favorite spot of river.
Same sun on our necks, arms self-consoling,
this is one warm *yes* for wholeness to another.

Mid-Day Hail

Inedible berries fill the wagon by the old thrift shop.
I have a similar facade, a breezy smile at each impasse,

a sense of *Go* even when the rusted swing says to stop.
What am I running from? Catapulting over tasks.

The truth leaves me blindsided beside the ant-covered grape,
where change is slow, almost invisible, but happening.

For days, unnoticed, the bluebird has been making its nest
in the garage. For years, my father, aging.

Missing is part of this lifestyle, and longing is its art.
Only certain attention seems to know this:

a turtle in the center of a rock in the sun,
its instinct to drop into water to escape me,

with my desperate thought that maybe a photo of it
will bring me closer to all that I've missed.

Pajama Drawer of Adolescence

The camouflage t-shirt, size extra small,
brings me to the day

the older boy with the gauges grips my waist,
times his car's revving with lights about to change.

In the passenger seat, I feel my lips should
be a certain shade of crimson.

Horizon line clearer, sky grayer, I decide
to ask him to let me out at the park, where Sam waits

wearing her own version of pretty: long, rainbow skirt,
brushing mulch beneath her swing.

Perpetually, it seems, we studied spiders' bell-shaped
webs on lilac flowers, the smoke and shape of boys' fireworks.

We could conceive of death but only to be sorry for it,
our own bodies growing lumpy and thin,

arms covered in hornet stings of empty touch,
not caring the way we needed.

Today, I am a dark statue, like the man before me.
I have stone parts and parts that fell off.

My hands make a circle while I frame the cloudy sun
for a painting which begins to look like arms of aloe

across a dark ravine. I call it,
blue tree of fog, self-lost or self-gained.

To Feel as Real as Each New Morning

My two fingerprints, smeared
on the inside of a frozen windshield,
drip with the fearlessness of child's fingerpaint—
I drive to the meadow, toggle of weeds and grasshoppers,
to feel life settle and start around me,
to feel like I'm part of it.

The way forgiveness is given makes a difference:
the dead elm branch
shatters on its way down,
or the silence of someone too far to hear.

For days, drawn to the redbud,
fuchsia born from its innermost root,
crusted with clear frost,
I open a small attic window for truth:
who have I been while stuck in some dream of *perfect*?

Lime Dogwood on Gray Sky

I found a new tulip today, tucked into its star-shape,
suffering a shine-down from an early moon.

I tried hard to quit pushing for an answer—
when all my fixing is done, it's time to fix you,

and, as quickly as the slick aviary of blackbirds
in your eyes blinks out the pain of my blaming,

I see I need to paint an access point back to myself.
If I might design such forgiveness, it would be, as a child,

when I resisted tearing open an early red tulip,
though so impatient for its full bloom,

or, last Sunday, when I found a lost beagle,
with a shredded paw like a marigold, itself—

rusty and metallic—and carried him home.

Broken Pot I Made

I will not make my silence look only like silence.
I will embody the cat statue, daisy lei, a mirror to her smile.
I will sit on the pile of violets with Gracie to avoid home.
Personify something, a wheat field, a plant: *saying nothing
is also a way of speaking*—a noncommittal *maybe*.

Or *Let's, Let's, Let's.* Let us take shape
in the finch, who squawks once close-by
then across the mountain. Let us be better at spotting
the trap of once-was before getting our feet caught.
Thinking back to an argument, I break the twig
the raccoon left on the table as an offering
like ripping a drawing of a family holding hands
by a child whose family never holds hands.

Let me, this time, be okay with imperfection,
sometimes a clatter of hand-painted porcelain
on concrete, the reality of a mistake—
thump of an everyday drum: merely an intro
that thrums even the soles of the feet.

Not Knowing What to Say

To shell out such a white sky, spring must be asking for a friend to face ob]
I have listened and not been listened to. I have tried to understand.

I get lost in the museum's tracings and what might be.
Instead of seeing the deep sense of *Go* like a banner over every day,

I imagine walking near a rainbowed puddle where even a stretch
is a kind of art: air escapes; the body becomes clay to shape and reshape.

Elsewhere in the mind, there is a falling out of love,
an inability that cements into a powerful silence.

At least, the mother spider on the porch keeps me company in this:
carrying a jetpack of eggs—an astronaut floating miles from earth.

Part of coming down is to quit looking for evidence:
this morning when your chest felt soft, like any human chest.

Thinking this, I stay in the garden when you call. You don't take offense.
We pass a look that says, *we might know each other again.*

ALL THE SALT SWELLING OF THE SEA LAUGHED ALOUD

after "Hymn To Demeter," trans. Jules Cashford

My light, foam paddleboard knocks against the wooden dock, and I fall the first time, baywater flooding my nostrils;

soft mud with fish parts and clam shells grabs my foot, and I do what you do on water:

repeat the same motion until maybe you're out of trouble.

In the distance, brown trees of Assateague, a razor of bug-eaten cedars, prove words for time powerless.

I hope that this version of quiet—

toes spreading sand in the wind of a wild horse's flicking tail,

the *ahm* of the park ranger when I reported the abandoned fawn by water's edge—

cures me of that youth where I felt like I could change you by trying

or could make a creature think better of us, hordes of pastels crowded to catch a glimpse

of eyes like mirrored worlds, of hooved feet born, unequivocally, from earth.

When We Look Out from the Pier

Gracie mouths the turning glowworm,
fast blink of neon green, wonders why
it stopped moving. This is like time,

mistaking her curiosity for fear:
the orange, leaf-soaked trail, pop of mushroom,
taste-worthy. Last trip here, I tried to dance with you

but felt that we could not compare
to the ribbon of midnight, stars and dried roses.
Yet I don't understand this conversation

between the snakeskin-draped trees, dark lake
blinking light, and our quiet tension,
but waiting has revealed itself as one way to listen.

Addition and Subtraction

Slipshod thunder, a parade of brave raindrops on the pane:
plenty of bothers these days—the tiptoed silk of a relative dying,

and the usual: trying to figure us out. Yesterday,
at the public pool: your chlorine lips cool on mine

let a childness take over: messy thick heart on the bottom
of the brush caddy we painted at the pottery shop.

I heard a boy lost in the woods when on the phone:
I don't want it, he said about his brother dying.

As you drape your cool arm on my side,
I wonder how the baby bird I saved from the road

could still be taken by the hawk,
when I did everything right to return it home,

tied a grass-lined basket to a tree, close to its nest.
Weather has its own way of misunderstanding:

lighting grabs the mountain like a soft apricot, splitting.

Logic as I Know It

Clovers peek at the sun; blue crabs scuttle
purposely forward without knowing.

I hold a broken berry, purple spread from finger to finger.
Gracie squeaks a yawn.

Her philosophy: stick your whole head in every ditch.
I want to tell the gas station clerk, *Look, I'm okay*.

And *let me expect a rainbow*.

You take me to the busiest beach but the emptiest spot.
We drop our secrets about what we really think along the ocean's edge.

The salt-breeze and sweat on my shoulders
feel like a drive-in movie about holding our lives in our own hands—

the final shot is a bird's eye:
beginning of the neighborhood kids, ending of the moon.

Cages for Plovers

On the balcony of the island house,
warm fog gathers on my binoculars,
making the world an ivory blur.

The food chain is less egrets-
snipping-krill but who has
the weapon with the most reach.

As much as I want to pet the wild ponies,
they remain ignorant, circling each other,
playing a square dance I cannot read.

Riptide stands between his pride and another;
Ace's Black Tie Affair mounts a mate.
It's all very impersonal.

Time wakes me next to you on the beach,
touching one balding spot, reciting
a dream about our impossibility.

The quiet dog of pathos swarms our feet
as we balance on rafts made to be balanced,
a lesson in protection and respect.

Plans

Fixed maples lean toward our house like large, skinny gods
who want answers. I want to reason with them: *isn't it enough*

to want to feel small again—to swish my hummingbird locket
back and forth on its chain, like a child swinging,

navy clouds of doubt by the goldenrod, a reminder
that gray finds its way even to the most objective:

a snail on the desert of a rock; me, you, all in one view
from above? This porch is foggy with webs, the swing,

rusted beyond hope. No one must have studied the range
of the swinging peony pot, nor checked which floorboards

to creak up to find bugs twirling in their mud. Here,
no one must have been a child, future spread open

like the field of abandoned bamboo at the center of town
that sounds like knocking in the wind.

Floor Findings

after "It's all I have to bring today" by Emily Dickinson

I am fine with an unclear *it*,
only until I think of all it could be—
forgiveness; stubbornness; not feeling worthy; an enameled lily;
the jelly bean by the dead ladybug on the office floor:
red husk of one year of travel
from stem-to-stem
beside a ball of sparkling pink sugar, dropped by a child.

I have spent the day in the land of the sky,
naming each porch design: steel broom by cobwebs,
shredded jay on stoop, metal watering can, tipped over.
A cat relieves me when it licks my hand.

To name is a version of hope, directing a painted bird
from a scrap of newspaper to a giant canvas.
It can be a promise to feel only my own sadness,
the way a mosquito does not drown
in sap but becomes its own jewel of amber.

Meanwhile, our Snowman Melts

In my dream, clay water builds new skin, fills cracks of guilt.
At the end of a ravine, there's a golden puddle of broken ice,
and I hold it in my gloved hands, let it melt,
and suddenly I am cushioned by snow, drawing wings.
I am looking for a steady thing to keep me here,
inside the world that seems to begin and end with your waking.
The deer that emerges, bearing the face of my dad,
says, *you become the sturdiness*. I wake to the sound
of cars doing their jobs—taking the city to work,
delivering messages from *used-to-be* homes:
I decide that to stay or to leave means, mostly, this.

Truth Color

Stars pulse in my memory of the night we drove to a park—
black air. White branches. My *I*, so lower-cased,
I could barely see it. In the room of your smile,
I was unbearable. Now: a deer stuck in my headlights—

yet I feel like I am the one spotted—
silence between us, on-looking.
Blue night traces the yellow knobs of her legs,
my tan arms like levers on the wheel of a metal ship.

Before this, I searched for answers in opposites:
Imagine or *Be real. Find safety* or *Be safe.*
In her narrow gaze, I am an animal, too,
tongue swimming, warm in the county of my mouth,

oval torsos on pegs, lashed eyes, spotlights on each other
who neither fight nor fly but keep looking.

About the Author

Christina Seymour is the author of the chapbook *Flowers Around Your Soft Throat* (Structo, 2016). Her poems also appear in Wick Poetry Center's touring exhibit, *Speak Peace—American Voices Respond to Vietnamese Children's Paintings*, housed at the War Remnants Museum in Vietnam; *The Moth*; *North American Review*; *Cimarron Review*; *The Briar Cliff Review*; and elsewhere. Her awards include the Russell MacDonald Creative Writing Award, scholarship at The Frost Place, and nominations for the Pushcart Prize, Best New Poets, and the AWP Intro Award. She teaches poetry and professional writing at Maryville College in Tennessee and for Johns Hopkins Center for Talented Youth online.

Glass Lyre Press

exceptional works to replenish the spirit

Glass Lyre Press is an independent literary publisher interested in technically accomplished, stylistically distinct, and original work. Glass Lyre seeks diverse writers that possess a dynamic aesthetic and an ability to emotionally and intellectually engage a wide audience of readers.

Glass Lyre's vision is to connect the world through language and art. We hope to expand the scope of poetry and short fiction for the general reader through exceptionally well-written books, which evoke emotion, provide insight, and resonate with the human spirit.

Poetry Collections
Poetry Chapbooks
Select Short & Flash Fiction
Anthologies

www.GlassLyrePress.com

www.ingramcontent.com/pod-product-compliance
Lightning Source LLC
Chambersburg PA
CBHW030131100526
44591CB00009B/607